Editor
Eric Migliaccio

Managing Editor
Ina Massler Levin, M.A.

Illustrator
Vicki Frazier

Cover Artist
Barb Lorseyedi

Art Production Manager
Kevin Barnes

Imaging
Rosa C. See

Publisher
Mary D. Smith, M.S. Ed.

GRADES K–2

MAY DAILY JOURNAL WRITING PROMPTS

MAY 3

MAY 8

MAY 26

Happy Mother's Day

Author

Maria Elvira Gallardo, M.A.

Teacher Created Resources, Inc.
6421 Industry Way
Westminster, CA 92683
www.teachercreated.com

ISBN-1-4206-3134-9

©2006 Teacher Created Resources, Inc.

Made in U.S.A.

Table of Contents

Introduction

More than ever, it is important for students to practice writing on a daily basis. Every classroom teacher knows that the key to getting students excited about writing is introducing interesting topics that are fun to write about. *May Daily Journal Writing Prompts* provides kindergarten through second-grade teachers with an entire month of ready-to-use journal topics, including special holiday and seasonal topics for May. All journal topics are included in a calendar that can be easily reproduced for students. A student journal cover allows students to personalize their journal for the month.

Other useful pages that are fun include:

⚜ A Blank Calendar (pages 6 and 7)

This can be used to meet your own classroom needs. You may want your students to come up with their own topics for the month, or it may come in handy for homework writing topics.

⚜ Word Banks (pages 40–43)

These include commonly-used vocabulary words for school, holiday, and seasonal topics. A blank word bank gives students a place to write other words they have learned throughout the month.

⚜ May Author Birthdays (page 44)

Celebrate famous authors' birthdays or introduce an author who is new to your students. This page includes the author's birthdays and titles of some of their most popular books.

⚜ May Historic Events (page 45)

In the format of a time line, this page is a great reference tool for students. They will love seeing amazing events that happened in May.

⚜ May Discoveries & Inventions (page 46)

Kindle students' curiosity about discoveries and inventions with this page. This is perfect to use for your science and social-studies classes.

Motivate your students' writing by reproducing the pages in this book and making each student an individual journal. Use all the journal topics included, or pick and choose them as you please. See "Binding Ideas" on page 48 for ways to put it all together. Planning a month of writing will never be easier!

Monthly Calendar

MAY

1	2	3	4
I want to give a bouquet of flowers to…	I can help animals by…	My teacher is important to me because…	If I could stay up all night…
9	**10**	**11**	**12**
Something I'm excited about is…	I think school uniforms are…	If children were in charge of the world…	If I could be on any TV show…
17	**18**	**19**	**20**
My favorite cousin is…	Friendship is important because…	I hope my next report card says…	It's not good to fight with people because…
25	**26**	**27**	**28**
As the weather gets warmer, I enjoy…	I'm excited it's almost summer because…	Having good manners is important because…	An animal I would love to pet is…

Monthly Calendar *(cont.)*

MAY

5	6	7	8
People celebrate Cinco do Mayo by…	During lunch, my friends and I talk about…	I take care of my body by…	It is important to celebrate mothers because…
13	**14**	**15**	**16**
I wish I had a million…	Soldiers are brave because they…	The last party I went to was…	I would like to interview…
21	**22**	**23**	**24**
When I can't get something I really want…	Veterinarians help animals…	The best time of day is…	I love cooking…
29	**30**	**31**	**Special Topic**
The craziest story I've ever heard is…	I can't wait for summer because…	Sometimes I wish I…	**Memorial Day** On Memorial Day, we remember…

Blank Monthly Calendar

MAY			
1	2	3	4
9	10	11	12
17	18	19	20
25	26	27	28

Blank Monthly Calendar *(cont.)*

M A Y

5	6	7	8
13	14	15	16
21	22	23	24
29	30	31	Free Choice Topic

I want to give a bouquet of flowers to

_____

_____

_____

_____

_____

                              _____

                              _____

                              _____

I can help animals by _____

_____

_____

_____

_____

_____

_____

_____

_____

My teacher is important to me because

_____

_____

_____

_____

_____

_____

_____

_____

If I could stay up all night _____

_____

_____

_____

_____

_____

_____

_____

_____

People celebrate Cinco de Mayo by

Feliz Cinco de Mayo!

During lunch, my friends and I talk about

_____

_____

_____

_____

_____

_____

_____

_____

I take care of my body by _____

_____

_____

_____

_____

_____

_____

_____

_____

It is important to celebrate mothers because

_____

_____

_____

_____

_____

_____

_____

_____

Something I'm excited about is _____

_____

_____

_____

_____

_____

_____

_____

_____

I think school uniforms are _____

_____

_____

_____

_____

_____

_____

_____

_____

_____

If children were in charge of the world

_____

_____

_____

_____

_____

_____

_____

_____

_____

If I could be on any TV show _____

_____

_____

_____

_____

_____

_____

_____

I wish I had a million _____

_____

_____

_____

_____

_____

_____

_____

_____

20

Soldiers are brave because they _____

_____

_____

_____

_____

_____

_____

_____

_____

The last party I went to was _____

_____

_____

_____

_____

_____

_____

_____

_____

_____

I would like to interview _____

_____

_____

_____

_____

_____

_____

_____

_____

_____

My favorite cousin is _____

_____

_____

_____

_____

_____

_____

_____

_____

_____

24

Friendship is important because _____

_____

_____

_____

_____

_____

_____

_____

_____

_____

I hope my next report card says _____

_____

_____

_____

_____

_____

_____

_____

_____

_____

It's not good to fight with people because

_____

_____

_____

_____

_____

_____

_____

_____

When I can't get something I really want

_____

_____

_____

_____

_____

_____

_____

_____

_____

Veterinarians help animals _____

_____

_____

_____

_____

_____

_____

_____

_____

The best time of day is _____

_____

_____

_____

_____

_____

_____

_____

_____

_____

I love cooking _____

_____

_____

_____

_____

_____

_____

_____

_____

As the weather gets warmer, I enjoy

_____

_____

_____

_____

_____

_____

_____

_____

I'm excited it's almost summer because

_____

_____

_____

_____

_____

_____

_____

_____

Having good manners is important because

_____

_____

_____

_____

_____

_____

_____

_____

_____

An animal I would love to pet is _____

_____

_____

_____

_____

_____

_____

_____

_____

The craziest story I've ever heard is

_____

_____

_____

_____

_____

_____

_____

_____

_____

I can't wait for summer because_____

_____

_____

_____

_____

_____

_____

_____

_____

Sometimes I wish I _____

_____

_____

_____

_____

_____

_____

_____

                                             _____

                                             _____

                                             _____

On Memorial Day, we remember _____

_____

_____

_____

_____

_____

_____

_____

_____

School Word Bank

alphabet	desks	map	recess
art	dictionary	markers	report card
assembly	encyclopedia	math	rules
award	folder	notebook	science
binder	glue	office	scissors
board	grades	paper	stapler
books	history	pencils	study
bus	homework	pens	teacher
children	journal	playground	thesaurus
class	learning	principal	write
crayons	lunch	reading	

Holiday Word Bank

May Holidays

Memorial Day

Mother's Day

Cinco de Mayo

Be Kind to Animals Week

National Teachers' Day

army	home	piñata
awareness	honor	protect
battle	humane	Puebla
brave	instruct	recognition
care	love	remember
classroom	mariachis	responsible
commemorate	matron	school
daughter	Mexico	soldiers
defend	military	sombrero
education	mommy	son
family	music	symbol
fiesta	observe	teach
fifth	parade	thank
flag	parent	unity
gifts	patriotism	victory
grandmother	pets	war

Seasonal Word Bank

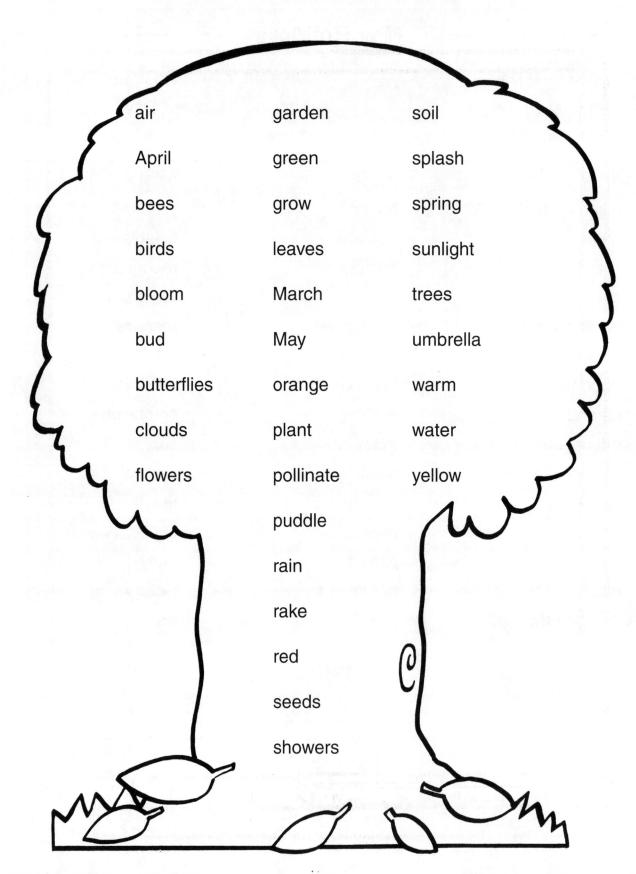

air	garden	soil
April	green	splash
bees	grow	spring
birds	leaves	sunlight
bloom	March	trees
bud	May	umbrella
butterflies	orange	warm
clouds	plant	water
flowers	pollinate	yellow
	puddle	
	rain	
	rake	
	red	
	seeds	
	showers	

42

My Word Bank

May Author Birthdays

3

Mavis Jukes

(b. 1947)

Alexander and the Terrible, Horrible, No Good, Very Bad Day (Antheum, 1972)

Sunday Morning (Atheneum, 1992)

5

Leo Lionni

(1910–1999)

Fish is Fish (Dragonfly, 1974)

Cornelius (Knopf, 1983)

Matthew's Dream (Knopf, 1991)

6

Ted Lewin

(b. 1935)

The Reindeer People (Simon & Schuster, 1994)

Gorilla Walk (HarperCollins, 1999)

6

Barbara McClintock

(b. 1955)

Heartaches of a French Cat (David R. Godine Publisher, 1989)

Dahlia (Farrar, Straus & Giroux, 2002)

10

Bruce McMillan

(b. 1947)

Eating Fractions (Scholastic, 1991)

The Baby Zoo (Scholastic, 1992)

My Horse of the North (Scholastic, 1997)

11

Peter Sis

(b. 1949)

Madlenka (Farrar, Straus & Giroux, 2000)

Ballerina! (Greenwillow, 2001)

12

Betsy Lewin

(b. 1937)

Cat Count (Henry Holt & Co., 2003)

Animal Snackers (Henry Holt & Co., 2004)

15

Eleanor Schick

(b. 1942)

Mama (Mama Cavendish, 2000)

I Am: I Am a Dancer (Marshall Cavendish, 2002)

16

Margaret Rey

(1906–1996)

Pretzel (Linnet Books, 1992)

Whiteblack the Penguin Sees the World (Houghton Mifflin, 2000)

20

Mary Pope Osborne

(b. 1949)

Dingoes at Dinnertime (Random House, 2000)

The Brave Little Seamstress (Atheneum/Anne Schwartz, 2002)

25

Barbara Bottner

(b. 1943)

Be Brown! (Grosset & Dumlap, 2002)

Charlene Loves to Make Noise (Running Press Kids, 2002)

29

Brock Cole

(b. 1938)

Larky Mavis (Farrar, Straus & Giroux 2001)

George Washington's Teeth (Farrar, Straus & Giroux, 2003)

May Historic Events

May 6, 1889

The Eiffel Tower was officially opened to the public at the Universal Exposition in Paris.

May 10, 1872

Victoria Woodhull became the first woman nominated for president of the United States.

May 10, 1908

Mother's Day was observed for the first time.

May 14, 1787

In Philadelphia, Pennsylvania, delegates began to write the Constitution for the United States.

May 15, 1918

The American Post Office Department (later renamed the USPS) began the first regular airmail service in the world.

May 17, 1954

The United States Supreme Court handed down a unanimous decision in *Brown v. Board of Education of Topeka, Kansas,* which outlawed racial segregation in public schools.

May 21, 1881

The American Red Cross was established by Clara Barton.

May 24, 1626

Peter Minuit bought Manhattan from the Algonkin Native Americans.

May 24, 1883

The Brooklyn Bridge in New York is opened to traffic after 14 years of construction.

May Discoveries & Inventions

3 **Christopher Columbus discovered Jamaica** on this date in 1494.

5 **In 1809 Mary Kies became the first woman to be awarded a U.S. patent.** Her patent was for a technique of weaving straw with silk and thread.

8 **A carbonated beverage that would be named "Coca-Cola" was invented** in 1886 by pharmacist Dr. John Styth Pemberton.

9 **The city of Reno, Nevada, was founded** in 1868.

10 **Christopher Columbus discovered the Cayman Islands** in 1503 and named them Las Tortugas after the numerous sea turtles there.

15 **The world's first machine gun was patented** in 1718 by James Puckle, a London lawyer.

16 **Root beer was invented** by Charles Elmer Hires in 1866.

17 **The saxophone was patented** by Adolphe Sax in 1846.

20 **A patent for blue jeans with copper rivets was granted** in 1873 to Levi Strauss and Jacob Davis.

22 **The Wright Brothers patented their aircraft** on this date in 1908.

24 **In 1844 the first electric telegram was sent** by Samuel F. B. Morse from Baltimore, Maryland, to Washington, D.C., saying "What hath God wrought?"

May

Journal

by

_____

Binding Ideas

Students will be so delighted when they see a month of their writing come together with one of the following binding ideas. You may choose to bind their journals at the beginning or end of the month, once they have already filled all of the journal topic pages. When ready to bind students' journals, have them color in their journal cover on page 47. It may be a good idea to reproduce the journal covers on hard stock paper in order to better protect the pages in the journal. Use the same hard stock paper for the back cover.

Simple Book Binding

1. Put all pages in order and staple together along the left margin.

2. Cut book-binding tape to the exact length of the book.

3. Run the center line of tape along the left side of the book and fold to cover the front left margin and the back right margin. Your book is complete!

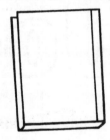

Yarn-Sewn Binding

1. Put all pages in order and hole-punch the left margin.

2. Stitch the pages together with thick yarn or ribbon.